© Hubert Germain-Robin 2012

Published by White Mule Press,
a division of American Distilling Institute
PO Box 577
Hayward, CA 94541

distilling.com/publications/books

All rights reserved.

No part of this book may be reproduced in any form or by any electronic or mechanical means including information storage and retrieval systems, without permission in writing from the author. The only exception is by a reviewer, who may quote short excerpts in a review.

Printed in the United States of America

ISBN 978-1-7369802-3-1

Traditional Distillation
Art & Passion

Hubert Germain-Robin

Contents

A History of Distillation 2

The Elements of Distilled Spirits 6

Vinification 12

The Alambic Pot Still 18

Distillation 28

Defects & Their Origins 38

General Advice 40

Cleaning the Still 44

Tasting 46

Conclusion 54

Appendices 56

Illustrations

A Diderot Pictorial Encyclopedia of Trades & Industry,
Denis Diderot; 1959
38

Ets. Chalvignac/Prulho, diagrams & text
20, 21, 24, 26, 27

L'Art de la Distillation, Jules Dujardin; 1855
2, 6, 12, 28, 40, 44, 46

La Vigne, Voyage Autour des Vins de France; 1878
18, 35, 51

Le Cognac; Jules Robin & Co.
11, 57

les 100 plus belles images du Cognac; 2007
viii, xxii, xxiii, 5, 36, 63

Original ink drawing by Jesse Okie
54

Cover painting by Michael Logan

Jules Robin & Co. Labels
15, 43

Ets. Robert Prulho S.A.
16 & 17

Foreword

Traditional Distillation—Art & Passion is an introduction to one of the oldest human endeavors – preserving the bounty of the summer. In this book (the first in a series of books on brandy production), Hubert Germain-Robin focuses on the essential elements – philosophical as well as technical – for the production of "*eau de vie,*" or water of life. Indeed, the true art of brandy distillation is to capture, in liquid form, the very essence of the Earth and its summer bounty. Some of us are born into distillation while for others, such as myself, the passion comes later in life. However, all passionate distillers share the same sense of connection between what we produce and the most basic elements of Earth, Water, Air and Fire, which we work with to capture the essence of the harvest, the *eau de vie*.

I have a special place in my heart for the brown spirits, those that take decades to truly develop new flavors by slow maturation in casks. These are the spirits that can emerge from the barrel after resting in darkness for years, to express a new self, a single spirit, formed by the combination of fruit and wood essences, married and transformed over the seasons. This is an important point, as there is a philosophical (and thus technical) divergence between producers of classic white *eau de vie* and *eau de vie* for brown spirits. In the former, the goal is to capture the flavor of fruit in a bottle, and of fruit that is the outward expression of summer's sun, the juicy sweetness of a ripe pear, or the mouth-watering tartness of a sour cherry. For brown spirits, we look to express the inner heart of the fruit and the season. It is a heart that is not as focused on the outward attractiveness of the youthful flower, but rather captures the inner beauty, a beauty as that expressed by the bristlecone pine, with its toe hold on the mountain, transformed by recording the passing seasons, century after century.

For any distiller, I believe it is important to understand the quality aspects of all spirits, be they cane, grain, or fruit based. My personal journey with classic distillation came by way of grain-based spirits. While I had been a wine and beer aficionado for many years and had been making all grain beers for some time, in the early 1980's I had the great fortune to take a Whiskey short course with the late Michael Jackson. Michael conveyed the great journey that brown spirits take after fermentation, and instilled in me a bug I have never been able to shake off. Yet, being in California at that time, the notion of producing a Scotch type (i.e. all barley) whiskey or whiskies at all, seemed to miss the point. California is the golden state, and the gold in this case is the blessing of fruit of exceptional quality and distinction. Thus, brandy!

However, in the early 1980's information on classical distillation and brandy production was almost impossible to come by and what literature existed was predominately in French. As such, I felt the need to visit and study in the great brandy regions of the world, Cognac, Armagnac, Calvados, Alsace, and the Black Forest. However, after spending many months over numerous trips I learned a few important things. For instance, while the big houses had equipment and techniques I was more familiar with (gas chromatography, adsorption spectroscopies, vibrational spectroscopies, and wet chemical laboratories), this is not where I found the great brandies. The truly great brandies were to be had in the small distilleries, many of which had handed down generation after generation the art and knowledge of great brandy production.

By the early 1980s I was beginning to have the sense that if I were to start a distillery in California, I would need to build everything from scratch. However, there were at that time only a few pioneers in California that had already taken on this task. The 1980s were a different time for craft spirits producers. When I asked one of the most respected wine merchants in California about the classic brandy made by Germain-Robin and my goal of starting a new distillery in California, the response was "Why would I buy a bottle of California brandy for $30 when I can get a bottle of great Cognac for the same price?" Yet, this was from someone who could extol the virtues of California wine, even in comparison with the great clarets of the Gironde. This was at a time when the domestic wine industry was on the rise and about to explode! Clearly, there were deep misunderstandings about what was and could be done with brandy production in the new world. It was then that I turned my attention back towards the West Coast and the first generation of distillers that took on, against all odds really, the early development of the craft distilling industry.

By the early 1980s Hubert Germain-Robin's idea of classic brandy production in the New World had led him to found Germain-Robin in Ukiah, CA. Other early craft distilling pioneers, such as Robert Léauté, came over from Cognac to build the now-defunct RMS facility in Napa, while Jorg Rupf, founder of St. George Spirits, was making classic fruit *eau de vie* in Alameda. By the mid 1980s, Steve McCarthy was just getting underway with Clear Creek in Oregon, and Randall Grahm had put together a distillery for *marc* and *eau de vie* production at the old Bonny Doon facility. This was the seed of the early craft distillery movement in the United States from which today's spectacular interest in craft spirits is derived. While some of these efforts have since fallen by the wayside, many have gone on to establish a new (or reborn) class of distilled spirit and a new "micro-"distillery industry.

I first met Hubert in the late 1980s when I convinced my sister, who was in the industry, to get me a tour of the old Germain-Robin facility at the Coale ranch. We were met by Ansley Coale, who then proceeded to give us the standard tour of "here is the still, here is the chai." At one point Ansley remarked that what Hubert was doing here is something new, and someday people will be making their way not to Europe, but here to California, to learn how to make great brandy. Did he know that I, in fact, was there to learn how to make brandies in the New World style that had been developed on that hill? After Ansley's 40 minutes with us was complete, it just so happened that Hubert was on his way to the chai. Ansley stated, "If you have any further questions you can address them to my partner." When Hubert arrived, I asked if he would mind answering a few more technical questions, to which he replied, "Of course not, what would you like to know?" I have been asking questions ever since, and Hubert has been continuously sharing his deep knowledge with me as well as the rest of the community.

This brings up another important point: in my experience, distillers around the world are open, engaging and helpful. However, I have heard some young members of the industry suggest that distillers are a closed bunch. I find that this comes mostly from a lack of knowing what to ask, or from talking to distillers that don't truly know themselves, and thus hide behind the "that is proprietary" answer.

Distilling is an art as well as a science, but it is the art which sets the great apart from the mediocre. In this light, it is easy to understand that no matter how much Cézanne could have explained how to paint a still life, few if any could have turned even the most open conversation into comparable work of their own. Thus, the artist has little to hide. While I find distilleries to be quite open, the barrels, pumps, and equipment are all in the open for anyone wishing to take notes. Yet, the real art of distillation, such as how and what decisions to make in producing brandies or other spirits, is in fact at the heart of conversations between distillers. It is here that this work fills a deep need.

What of those wishing to learn this art, yet who are unable to make the trip to visit the studios/distilleries of those artists who understand the process? Before this work, there was little else one could do save going to a university library, and then one would need to understand or learn a foreign language (since most of the works on brandy production are from Europe), only to find these volumes more technical renditions of the process. One can also search the Internet for scraps of information, but many times these are far removed from the primary source. Now, with this work, Hubert Germain-Robin, one of the greatest distillers of the late 20th and 21st century, has opened the world of distillation of fruit wines to a new generation of distillers, potential distillers, and further, to all lovers of the spirits of the summer.

This work is focused on the art and techniques of *eau de vie* production for spirits of great length and finesse – spirits that are built to age and develop over many decades. As such it is a work that will be referred to over and over as the art of the distiller progresses. The information here comes from a deep understanding of the quality factors of world-class brandies, and the aspects of production that influence their birth in the distillery. It is focused on the processes in the vineyard, winery, and distillery, and does not address the other important aspects of brown spirits production, such as the aging and blending processes, which we can only hope will be the focus of future efforts by Hubert. What we have here is a guide, and less of a "how-to" book. Rather, it is more of an insightful musing on the fundamental aspects of *eau de vie* production that, if considered deeply, will provide the basis not only for the techniques of fine brandy production but, more importantly, the thinking and guiding philosophy of classic brandy production.

Daniel L. Farber
Osocalis Distillery
Santa Cruz, California, 2012

Introduction

he art of distillation has finally caught up with philosophy, poetry and mysticism, all of which historically have played primordial roles in the elaboration of fine spirits. The gentle extraction of fruits, plants, minerals and other elements during the slow process of double distillation allows the distiller to concentrate with infinite care the essences of the base material. These essences can contain fruity notes, spicy elements or deep mineral accents, depending on the origin, the weather and growing conditions. Each fractional characteristic comes together to personalize the integrated end product.

Distillation can be the expression of fresh ingredients or it can be a step to aging and blending, which creates an altogether different result. An artistic sensibility and a sense of vision, added to common sense and experience, are the roots of your creation. Inspirations elevate your passion for the craft and ignite a quest to develop the perfect distilling technique.

Élévation

Au dessus des étangs, au-dessus des vallés,
Above the valleys and the lakes: beyond
Des montagnes, des bois, des nuages, des mers,
The woods, seas, clouds and mountain ranges: far
Par delà le soleil, par delà les éthers,
Above the sun, the aethers silver-swanned
Par delà les confins des sphères étoilées,
With nebulae, and the remotest star,

Mon esprit, tu te meus avec agilité,
My spirit! with agility you move
Et, comme un bon nageur qui se pâme dans l'onde,
Like a strong swimmer with the seas to fight,
Tu sillonnes gaiement l'immensité profonde
Through the blue vastness furrowing your groove
Avec une indicible et mâle volupté.
With an ineffable and male delight.

Envole-toi bien loin de ces miasmes morbides;
Far from these foetid marshes, be made pure
Va te purifier dans l'air supérieur,
In the pure air of the superior sky,
Et bois, comme une pure et divine liqueur,
And drink, like some most exquisite liqueur,
Le feu clair qui remplit les espaces limpides.
The fire that fills the lucid realms on high.

Derrière les ennuis et les vastes chagrins
Beyond where cares or boredom hold dominion,
Qui chargent de leur poids l'existence brumeuse,
Which charge our fogged existence with their spleen,
Heureux celui qui peut d'une aile vigoureuse
Happy is he who with a stalwart pinion
S'élancer vers les champs lumineux et sereins;
Can seek those fields so shining and serene:

Celui dont les pensées, comme des alouettes,
Whose thoughts, like larks, rise on the freshening breeze
Vers les cieux le matin prennent un libre essor,'
Who fans the morning with his tameless wings,
—Qui plane sur la vie, et comprend sans effort
Skims over life, and understands with ease
Le langage des fleurs et des choses muettes!
The speech of flowers and other voiceless things.

— *Charles Baudelaire*

How I Became a Distiller

I was born on the property of my grandfather, Jacques Germain-Robin at the Chateau du Logis de Lafon, which is situated near the town of Cognac, France. My family has been established in the Cognac region since 1605. They were important members of the Royal Administration and purchased many different properties around Cognac. Since 1782, we have been distillers and merchants under the name of Jules Robin and Cie. They developed important trades, especially in the Far East, Europe, and in both North and South America.

My profile is somewhat atypical because I started working with aged spirits, then [went backwards] to learn about distillation, and finally about vinification and viticulture. As a teenager during school breaks, I was working either in the cellar or at the bottling line.

Later on, as a young man, I became interested in the distillation process, so I took the courses at the Fondation Fougerat School of Distillation of the Station Viticole de Cognac. Under the direction of Master Distiller Yvon Courlit, along with three other students, I learned the principles of double distillation on two small alembics of 160 gallons. One was fired with wood and coal, the other was fired with propane. The wood and coal-fired alembic requires a lot of experience to learn how to build and keep a constant fire of consistent temperature. The dryness and hardness of the wood, and the size and nature of the coal have to be taken into consideration. With the gas burner, adjustments are precise and punctual, plus the environment is much cleaner. At that point in my distilling education, my destiny was foretold by a growing passion for the art of distillation.

Following my apprenticeship, and in order to perfect my knowledge, I distilled in the different areas of the Cognac region to learn the methods of distillation required by the different houses of Cognac. Each of them has strict requirements by which they reproduce with consistency their own traditional recipe.

When I came to California in 1981, I realized the unbelievable potential of the New World, with such diversity in grape varietals, microclimates, and less demanding restrictions than there are in France. In the following years, I found a small antique alembic that I shipped to California, along with used and new barrels. I also followed the course of tasting at the Organisation Economique du Cognac, under the guidance of Master Taster Pierre-Alain Gardrat. I learned each precise step of production under the direction of Master Blender Pierre Frugier at Martell Cognac. I then built a shed in the mountains of Mendocino County to shelter the pot still, and finally in 1983, I started distilling my first Pinot Noir and French Colombard.

A History of Distillation

istillation is a very old technique which was used by the Chinese 3,000 years BC, the East Indians 2,500 years BC, the Greeks 1,000 years BC, and the Romans 200 years BC. In the beginning, all of the above cultures produced a liquid, later called alcohol by the Arabs, which was used for medicinal purposes and to make perfumes.

By the sixth century AD, the Arabs had started to invade Europe and brought with them the technique of distillation. Chemists and monks progressively improved both the technique and distillation equipment. In 1250, Arnaud de Villeneuve was the first to distill wines in France; he called the product that resulted from this process "*eau de vie*" or water-of-life. He attributed to it the virtue of prolonging life.

Today, the pot still used in the Cognac area is known as the charentais pot still. "Ambix" is a Greek word defined as a vase with a small opening. This vase was part of the distillation equipment. Eventually, Arabs changed the word "Ambix" to "Ambic" and called the distillation equipment "Al Ambic." Later in Europe, the word was changed to Alambic.

The Dutch, French, Irish, Scots and others started producing distilled spirits around the 15th and 16th century. They created gin (Holland), whiskey (Scotland and Ireland), Armagnac and Cognac (France).

Since the capacity of the still depended on the raw material of the distillation, the shape was related to the country which used the distillation equipment. In the Cognac region, around 1600, the "Chevalier de la Croix marron" perfected *eau de vie* through double distillation. In France, Chaptal (1780) and Adam (1805) substantially improved the efficiency of distillation, and gave the pot still its final design. The Cognac makers, continually seeking to produce the best quality Cognac, brought both the pot still design and the double distillation methods to peaks of perfection.

In North America, bourbon and whiskey were first produced around 1750. In the booklet "America Brandy Land," published by the California Brandy Advisory Board, the Mission San Fernando produced around 2,000 barrels of brandy during the 1830s. Father Duran, the brandy maker at the Santa Barbara mission, produced double distillation brandy.

Progressively during the 1950s, most brandy producers gave up distilling. Those who continued to distill preferred using the column still because of its ability to produce a brandy compatible to the consumer trend.

The Way And Spirit Of Distillation

"Being in a good spirit makes better spirit."

In practicing the art of distillation, there are several factors that will help you to perfect the craft and to create a better spirit. For instance, it is important to always be steady and smooth in adjusting the settings on the still's burner in order to avoid turbulence in the pot. Brisk changes in the flame will result in a difficult sorting out of the different components.

Another factor that affects the final spirit is making sure to do slow and clean cuts from the heads to the *eau de vie* (EDV), and then again from the EDV to the *secondes*.

Just as it is important to know what to do to create good spirit, it is equally important to know what not to do in distillation. If one does not know how to distill properly, the consequences can be dangerous, if not fatal. For example, in the mid-1950s, my father Henri Germain-Robin was traveling in Borneo in Indonesia to sell his cognac. While visiting a local distillery with his agent, they tasted the products. After all, it was important to be polite to his hosts and not refuse.

When he returned to his hotel shortly thereafter, he was not feeling well. He went blind for half an hour! Fortunately, he recovered from this dangerous experience. Most likely the culprit of his blindness was in the poor quality of the base product. The distiller did not cut the heads, thus leaving such toxins as methanol, ethyl acetate, and other low boiling point esters in the spirit.

The Elements of Distilled Spirits

Grapes & Terroir

By addressing grapes (or other ingredients), you are determining the base of what will be your final product. The notion of terroir in winemaking is an indefinable essence, a gift that the land gives to the grapes, fruits, grains or roots, which in turn create a wide range of aromas and tastes. What Nature has to offer through any particular conditions will first determine the personality of your distillate.

The importance of the soil's role has been demonstrated for centuries. It brings complexity, longevity and harmony in the end product. Density of limestone, proportion of clay, presence of sand, loam, rocks, granite, fossils, etc., are "primordial" and are an important contribution in the character of the fruit and plants with mineral accents. Other factors that affect the final result include drainage of soil, planting on the slope of a hill or in a valley, and whether planting is close to a river or upon hill tops.

Microclimate

In addition to the soil, the grapes are heavily influenced by the microclimate in which they grow. Along with other elements, there is also exposure to the sun and moonlight, rain precipitation, percentage of humidity in the air, storms, wind, maritime influences, elevation of land, and pollution. Each micro-environment has its own unique set of insects, birds and animals that roam the land. And of course, the culture of the people who have been living and taking care of the land since the beginning of time also affects the final product.

In coastal areas, planting in locations near the ocean gives a saltiness that is detrimental to fruit brandies, but is perhaps more appropriate to grain spirits.

Cultivation & The Quality Of The Grapes

In the vineyards, one must consider the orientation of planting, the space between the vines, the width of the rows, and the types of pruning. Other factors include the age of the vine, the number of grape bunches per vine, the type of fertilizer (organic or not) that is added to the soil, and other products that are sprayed on the foliage and fruits. Depending on the particular weather due to the latitude and longitude of the vineyard, the application of wettable sulfur could be damaging to quality if applied too close to harvest time. For example, in

Cognac, Armagnac, and Calvados, rains during the summer command later spraying to avoid mildew and rots, but in drier regions, it is not necessary. In hot and sunny California, my personal preference is to forbid any application of wettable sulfur after the 4th of July.

Varietals

Throughout my career as a distiller in France and California, I experimented with over 40 different varieties of both red and white grapes. I discovered that some are more suitable than others for distillation. White grapes are usually more desirable for distillation because of their freshness, better acidity, and more mineral influences. Red varietals should always be processed in a "blanc de noir" method, with skin contact kept to an absolute minimum in order to avoid tannins and color, which lower the organoleptic quality of the distillates.

I have also discovered that the assemblage of the final blend dictates what type of varietals one chooses to distill. It is at this point that the distiller's choices will affect the final blend – it is where the "roots" of the blend originate, and the distiller's vision is critical. It is a turning point, because every decision the distiller makes will affect the final product. The distiller must think through what qualities he or she would like to achieve, such as what will be the proportion of fruit to floral, spice, or other characteristics. It depends on what they envision, where they live, and what their tastes are in life. This is where the artistry of the process begins; distillers reveal their soul and creativity at this point.

Your choice of varietals should take into account their affinities and their complementarities. If you plan to create blends of different eaux de vie later, you need good balance and harmony between the different elements of head, body and finish supported by a firm structure. This is ultimately a question of subjectivity and vision. Many different vineyard elements should be taken in consideration, such as clone, terroir, age of the vines, etc.

If you prefer to use a single varietal, your goal will be to extract the essence of this specific varietal/clone of grape from each particular vineyard. With distillation, you can lower or elevate some of the elements by cautiously changing the distillation speed and/or making changes to the cuts. For instance, if using an aromatic varietal such as Viognier and Muscat, you would want to take off more heads during the second distillation.

Grapes Tried On An Alambic

White Varietals:

French Colombard: Floral, spicy, good acidity.

Chenin Blanc: Fragile, short.

Chardonnay

Burger

Sauvignon Blanc: Nervous, spicy, sometimes mineral.

Sauvignon Vert (Muscadelle)

Pinot Blanc

Pinot Gris

Gewurztraminer: Rose, lychee, tropical spices, musky, looses acidity with ripeness, can be oily and bitter.

Ehrenfelzer (Riesling/Sylvaner)

Riesling (California character): Nervous, floral, noble, peach, apricot skin.

Semillon: Citrus, lanolin, round, full, viscous, very good aging potential.

Palomino

Golden Chasselas

Viognier: Needs to be ripe to express its character; nice body, flowery, very complex, honey, peach, apricot, violet, almonds, exotic.

Marsanne

Rousanne

Ugni Blanc

Folle Blanche

Muscat: (petit gran/canelli) Musky, very aromatic, ripe peach or orange peel, exuberant, can be harvested at an early stage.

Green Hungarian

Red Varietals:

(Must be vinified like "blanc de noir" and have minimum skin contact to avoid color and tannins)

- Pinot Noir: Structure is noble, racy, feminine, deep, complex, red berries, raspberry, leather, violet, truffle, difficult temper.
- Gamay Beaujolais
- Napa Gamay (Valdiguie)
- Merlot
- Carbernet Sauvignon
- Syrah
- Petite Sirah
- Zinfandel
- Sangiovese
- Grenache: Robust, muscular, productive, high in alcohol, tends to be aggressive.
- Cinsault
- Primitivo

Cold Climate, Hardy Grapes (-20F/-29C):

- Frontenac
- Frontenac Gris
- La Crescent
- Seyval Blanc
- La Crosse
- Edelweiss
- St. Pepin

Harvest

The goal when the grapes are destined for distillation is not to pick them at full maturity. Like champagne and sparkling wine, you want to have a strong level of acidity, low pH for crispness, and low alcohol for more concentration. The riper the grapes, the less finesse and delicateness the spirit will have. The sugar range of the grapes should be between 18 to 22 degree brix in order to obtain a wine between nine and 11 percent alcohol by volume.

The decision of harvest timing depends upon several factors, such as the varietal, the particularity of the vineyard, and the number of tons per acre. It should be noted, however, that some aromatic varietals such as Viognier are more unusual in that they do not show their potential and a beautiful nose until a later maturity (23 degree brix). On the other hand, Muscat, Riesling, and Gewurtztraminer will show their aromatic potential at an early stage.

Much attention and care should be given to every detail of the harvest. There are three points at which this is especially true. First, the time of day the grapes are picked is very significant. If possible, it is best to pick them earlier in the day. Next, great care should be taken to make sure that leaves, rocks, vine shots, and other undesirable elements do not find their way into the crop. Finally, larger picking containers cause more broken grape clusters, resulting in deterioration and oxidation of the fruit. It is important also to avoid leaving the bins to bake in the sun or soak in the rain before crushing and pressing.

La vendimia se verifica en Septiembre y Octubre, dando lugar á grandes fiestas. Cuando el zumo de la vid, prensado en las cubas, ha sido transformado en un vino claro y límpido, este vino es enviado á las destilerías.

Vinification

D'après les Planches de l'Encyclopédie 1763

Alembic	Athanor	Bain Vapeur	Bain Marie	Chopine
Cucurbite	Distiller	Eau	Eau courante	Eau de Vie
Esprit de Vin	Esprit	Fien de cheval	Filtrer	Lampe
Oeuf Philosophique	Pinte	Quinte Essence	Retorte	Sublimer
Tartre	Verre	Vin	Vinaigre	Vinaigre blanc
Vinaigre distillé	Vinaigre rouge	Vin Blanc	Vin Rouge	Lut de Sapience

Caracteres de Chymie.

owadays, with the amazing choice of yeasts on the market, the distiller has many more possibilities to influence or change fermentations by enhancing more fruitiness, floral accents or traces of minerals.

Wines intended for distillation must be perfect, because a slight defect that is hardly detectable in the wine may be detectable in the *eau de vie*. This is because of the intensity of concentration that occurs during double distillation.

Pressing

Most types of presses will do the job of crushing with good results. However, the continuous screw press is forbidden in brandy production. It is too hard on the grapes and results in a great deal of vegetative and green aromas from the stems and skins, and an oily character that comes from the crushing of the seeds.

The number of gallons per ton you can expect to obtain for a good quality wine will vary on varietals, size of cluster, exposure, and year. The range should be between 155 to 175 gallons per ton of juice.

Absolutely NO sulfur should be added before or during fermentation – otherwise it will bond with the juice or wine. The result of adding sulfur would create a sensation of burnt odors in the nose and on the palate. If refrigeration is not possible after fermentation is complete, then as a last alternative, a small dose of sulfur can be used to protect the wine from oxidation.

Tanks

Stainless steel tanks with refrigeration are recommended to be able to control the temperature. Through the duration of fermentation, 60 to 65 degrees F is recommended.

Fermentation (& The Lees)

The choices of cultivated yeast have been expanded greatly over the last decades. You can now give all types of character to wines through different yeast strains. For example, you can transform a Sauvignon Blanc to give it a Chardonnay character. My personal preference of yeast is for the soft ones, such as "cote de blanc" or natural wild yeasts, which adds more complexity to a spirit destined for long-term aging. I would not recommend using wild yeasts for short-term aging because the fruit is more subdued and less forward.

Wines should be fermented with the light lees, except in bad years or if a defect is detected. Light lees in small quantity are beneficial most of the time, except when defects due to poor quality of the ingredients or to vinification problems. They bring a spicy richness and depth. During aging they can be a great combination with the oak tannins.

Malolactic fermentation is not suitable for all varietals. It shortens the nose but will lend a buttery creaminess (in combination with the lees) during the aging process by giving a good mouth feel on the palate and fatness in the structure. Some varietals that work well with malolactic fermentation are Semillon, Colombard, Chenin Blanc. Those that don't work as well with malolactic fermentation are Pinot Noir, Gamay, and Sauvignan Blanc.

If you decide to use malolactic fermentation, the easiest way to start it is in the middle of the alcohol fermentation because of the warmer temperature. It is also a factor for the protection of the wine against microbial infections.

After fermentation, keep the wine on the lees. The lees are slowly releasing CO_2, which is good for conservation. Bring the temperature down to 40 degrees F – the colder the better – if you are not distilling it immediately. If you have headspace in your tanks, the use of nitrogen works best because it is neutral and it dissipates. A small dose of sulfur also can be used with caution.

When transporting the wine from the winery to your distillery, you will need to stir the lees from the bottom of the tank to put them in suspension. They can often become packed at the bottom of the tank, and without manual agitation, pumping will not be enough to get them out. Traditionally, a *rouable*, a rake-like tool with a long wooden stick and a board attached to one end, is used to stir the lees from the top opening of the tank. The wooden stick should be about five feet longer than the length or height of the tank in order to maximize stirring capacity. This is the most efficient way to put the lees into suspension. Once the lees are well agitated, pump the wine out by the bottom valve before the lees settle down again.

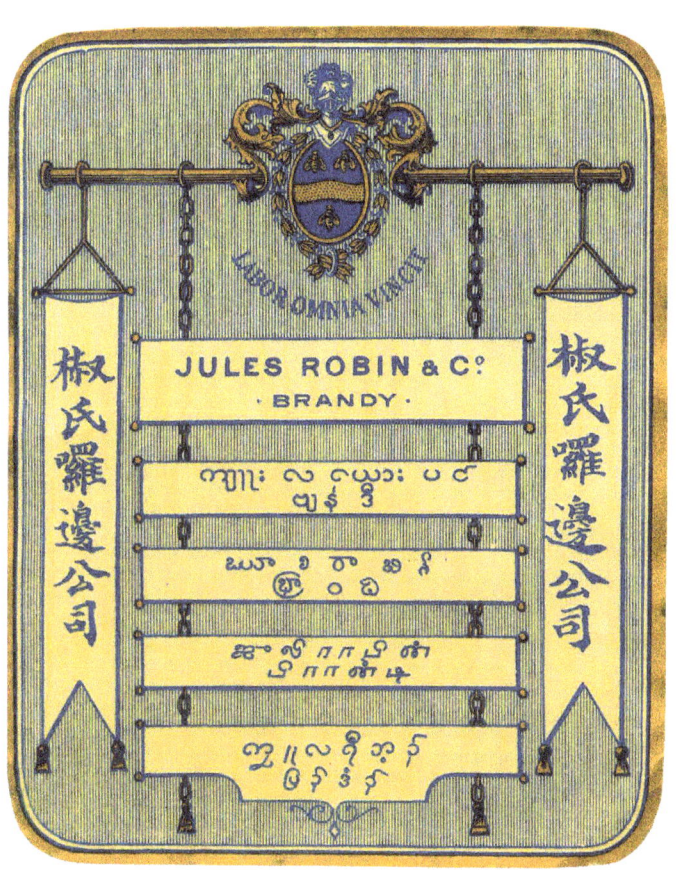

NAMES OF THE PARTS WHICH GO TO MAKE UP A CHARENTAIS ONION SHAPED STILL

	CHARENTAIS STILL			ACCESSORIES
	without wine	with wine		
Ⓐ Cucurbit (pot)	.	.	㉕	Alcoholmeter holder
Ⓑ Head	.	.	㉑	Steel cone
Ⓒ Swan-neck	.	.	㉒	Pyrex sight glass
Ⓓ Wine		.	㉓	Cooling funnel
Ⓔ Coil	.	.	㉔	Thermostatic valve
Ⓕ Cooler	.	.	㉕	Water spray ball
① Drain valve	.	.	㉖	Inox valve
② Level sight glass	.	.	㉗	Still flushing cock valve
③ Level cock valve		.	㉘	Thermometer
④ Collar of cucurbit	.	.	㉙	Bronze box
⑤ Collar of swan-neck	.	.	㉚	Reception tank for head of distillate
⑥ Bayonet coupling			㉛	Gas burner
⑦ Charging valve		.	㉜	Gas safety control panel
⑧ By-pass valve		.	㉝	Cast iron
⑨ By-pass		.	㉞	Hearth
⑩ Bronze Y-fitting		.	㉟	Register
⑪ Level sight glass		.	㊱	Draught moderator
⑫ Cap		.	㊲	Chimney
⑬ Thermometer		.	㊳	General stove setting

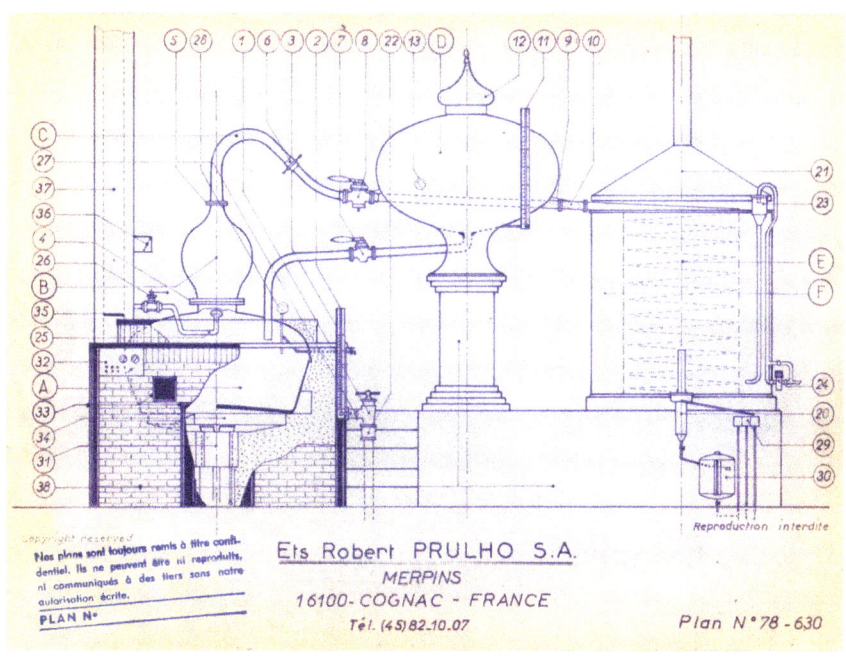

The Alambic Pot Still

Cognac pot still is made of copper and brass. Some of the pot still parts that are less important to the quality of the Cognac or brandy (e.g. valves, pipings, condenser tank) can be made in stainless steel for practical reasons. However, copper remains the most efficient metal to build pot stills.

Copper offers the following advantages: it is malleable, it is a good conductor of heat, it resists corrosion from fire and wine, it reacts with wine components such as sulfur components and fatty acids (this property is always favorable for the quality of Cognac or brandy), and it is a catalyst for favorable reactions between wine components.

Copper boiler (A)

When the boiler is filled with 2,500 liters of wine, the head space above is around 490 liters. The boiler is the main part of the pot still, and it is specially built to withstand continuous direct flame of approximately 1500º C. The inside of the boiler is well polished so that the copper presents a smooth surface for easy cleaning.

The boiler is in constant contact with the direct flame fed by natural gas, propane or butane. Boiler equipment includes the pipe to fill the boiler, the vent pipe, the boiler cleaner, and the valve to empty the boiler. *(figure 1A, page 20)*

Hat (B)

This part of the pot still is located directly above the boiler. The volume of the hat is approximately 10 to 12 percent of the capacity of the boiler, depending on the specifications required by the distiller.

The shape and the volume of the hat determine the concentration, selection and separation of the different volatile components. This selection process occurs when volatile compounds condense in the hat and fall down again in the boiler, where they must be re-distilled upwards. This phenomenon is called the reflux process. *(figure 2B page 20)*

Swan's Neck (C)

This part of the pot still is curved like a swan's neck and drives the vapor into the coil. The height and the curve of the swan's neck are extremely important to the reflux process. *(figure 3C, page 20)*

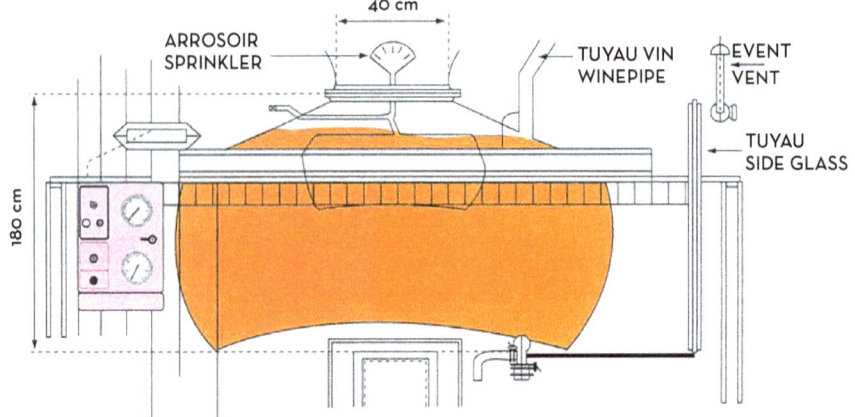

Fig 1A | *Chaudière cuivre* | copper boiler

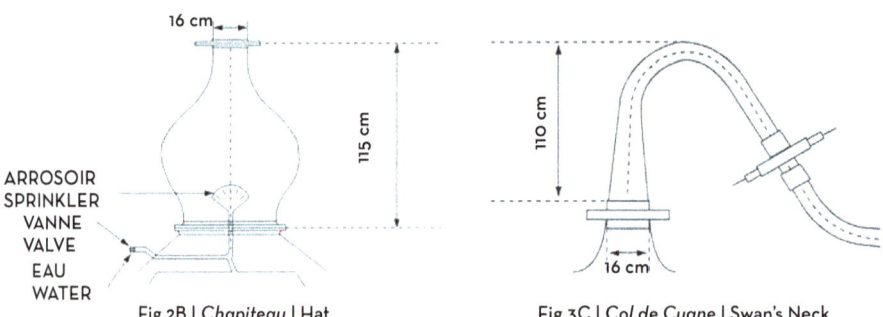

Fig 2B | *Chapiteau* | Hat

Fig 3C | *Col de Cygne* | Swan's Neck

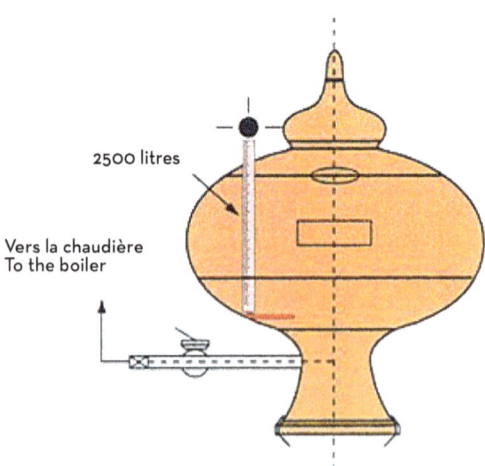

Fig 4D | The Wine Pre-Heater

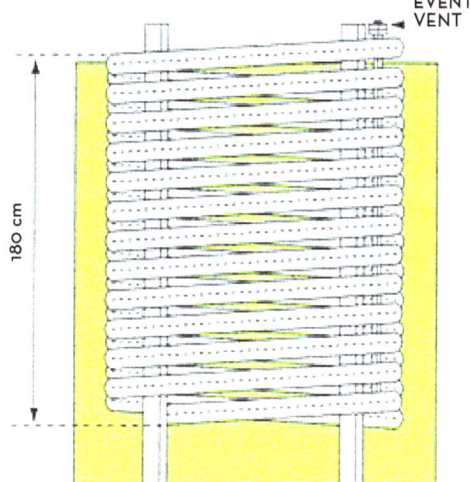

Fig 5E | *Serpentin* | Coil

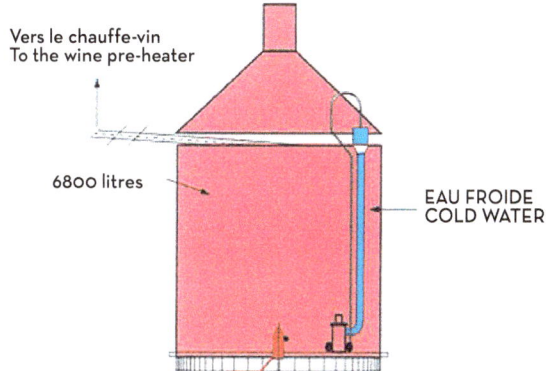

Fig 6F | *Condenseur* | Condenser

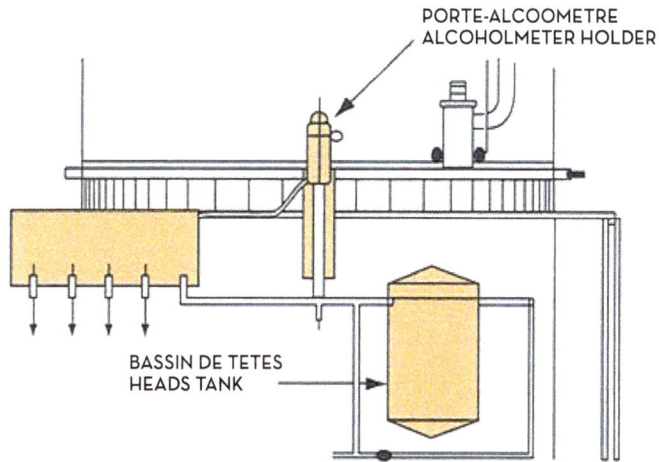

Fig 7G | Porte-Alcométre | Alcoholmeter Holder

Wine Pre-Heater (D)

This is the economical part of the pot still. The swan's neck pipe runs through the wine pre-heater and around its back. During the first hours of distillation, we refill the wine pre-heater for the next cycle. By directing the hot vapors through the wine pre-heater the wine can be pre-heated for the next distillation. The alternative pipe running around the outside of the pre-heater is used when the temperature of the contents of the wine pre-heater is sufficient. This will avoid overheating the contents of the wine pre-heater. *(figure 4D, page 20)*

Coil (E)

The coil pipe is also made of copper. During condensation, the copper reacts to the components of the distillate (sulfur components and fatty acids) to give insoluble combinations. These combinations are removed from the distillate by filtration when they reach the alcoholmeter holder. The coil has two functions: to condense the steam and to cool the distillate to a proper temperature for filtration. To facilitate condensation, the coil diameter is larger at the beginning of the coil and becomes smaller until it reaches the alcoholmeter holder. *(figure 5E, page 21)*

Condenser (F)

This is a cylindrical tank made of copper or stainless steel, which contains the copper coil pipe. Its capacity is around 6,800 liters. The condenser is filled with water during the distillation. Cold water enters into the condenser at the bottom, while the hot water heated during the condensing process comes out of the top of the condenser. *(figure 6F, page 21)*

Alcoholmeter Holder (G)

The alcoholmeter port is also made of copper and has several different purposes: to filter the distillates; to check the temperature; to check the alcohol content of what will be a Cognac or brandy; to offer an access point to the distiller; and to check the progress of the distillation. *(figure 7G, page 21)*

Heads Tank (H)

This is a small stainless steel tank (50 liters capacity) used to collect the first part of the distillate, called the heads.

Gas Burner (I)

The gas burner is equipped with the pilot flame and a reliable security system. The most commonly used fuels are propane, butane and natural gas. The gas panel to control the burner is located at the front of the pot still. Under the boiler, the temperature reaches around 1500 degrees C. This high temperature is essential to heat and to cook the wine to create aromas during the distillation process.

The Double Distillation
Variations of the Alcohol Content

Example with origination wine at 10% alcohol by volume:

First Distillation

The distillate is separated in three fractions: heads, hearts or *brouillis*, and tails. The alcohol content of the distillate is around 60% (alc./vol.) in the first fraction and reaches 0% (alc./vol.) at the end of the first distillation. *(figure 8, page 24)*

Second Distillation

The distillate is separated in four fractions: heads, hearts 1 or Cognac (or brandy), hearts 2, or *secondes* and tails. The alcohol content of the distillate is around 80% (alc./vol.) in this first fraction and reaches 0% (alc./vol.) at the end of the second distillation. *(figure 9, page 24)*

During the second distillation, the curves are slightly different because of the increased alcohol contents of the *brouillis*. The heating program established for distillation of wine and *brouillis* can certainly influence the concentration of components in the distillates. Higher heat is favorable for the less volatile components, as it will allow them to distill earlier and to be present in the first fractions of the distillation in higher concentration.

Distillation Process
Three distillation processes exist in the Cognac area, the most common one follows:

A first distillation of wine gives 3 fractions: heads, hearts (*brouillis*) and tails. Heads and tails are re-distilled with the following batch of wine. The *brouillis* is used for the second distillation, also called "*bonne chauffe.*"

A second distillation of *brouillis* gives four fractions: heads, hearts 1 (cognac), heart 2 (*secondes*) and tails. Heart and tails are re-distilled with *brouillis*.

[Note] The mixture remaining in the boiler after distillation is known as "stillage." This de-alcoholized solution must be treated to avoid contamination.

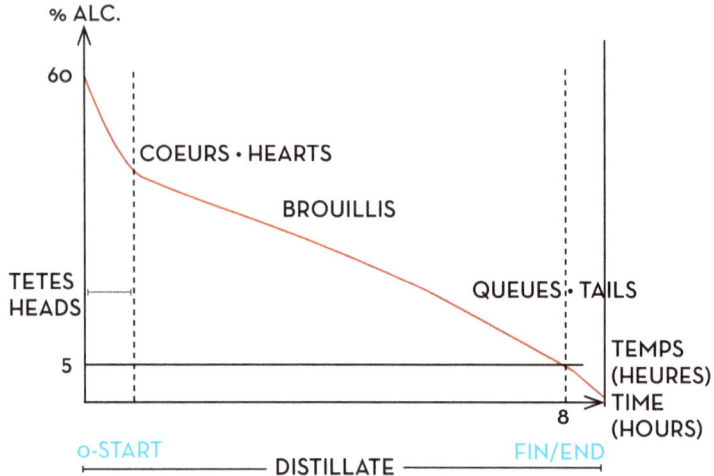

Fig 8 | Premiére Distillation (vin) | First Distillation (wine)

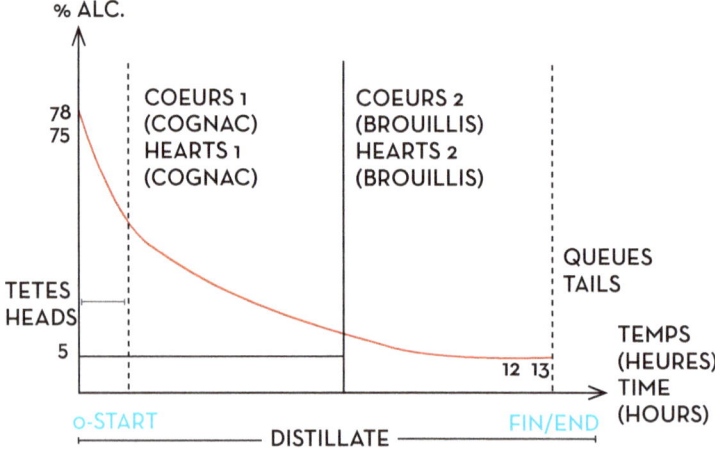

Fig 9 | Seconde distillation (brouillis) / Second distillation (brouillis)

The first distillation "brouillis" production

The running time:

> To remove the stillage
> To clean the pot still 30mn
> To fill the boiler with wine 30mn
> Time to reach boiling point 1h, 30mn
> Heads 30mn
> *Brouillis* 6h, 30mn
> Tails 1hr, 30mn
> **Total** **11h, 00mn**

Each fraction is obtained at a temperature below 15ºC. In this case they are removed by filtration combinations between sulfury components and copper and a part of the fatty acids and copper. *(figure 10a, page 26)*

The second distillation or "bonne chauffe"

The running time:

> To remove the stillage
> To clean the pot still 30mn
> To fill the boiler with brouillis 30mn
> Time to reach boiling point 1h, 30mn
> Heads 30mn
> Cognac/Brandy 6h, 00mn
> Seconds 4h, 00mn
> Tails 1hr
> **Total** **14h, 00mn**

Heads are obtained between 16ºC and 18ºC and seconds and tails below 15ºC like the *brouillis* during the first distillation. *(figure 10b, page 27)*

Cutting data: Generally wine for distillation in the Cognac area contains 7% to 9% alcohol, depending on the harvest conditions of the year.

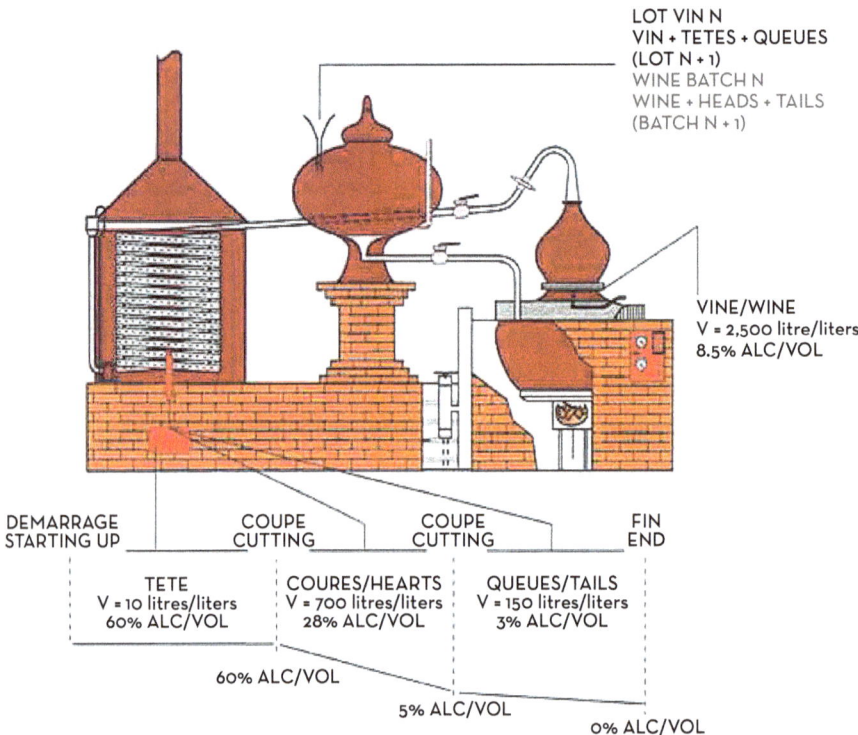

Fig 10a: Seonde distillation - bonne chauffe - production de cognac ou de brandy - temps de fonctionnement 14 heures environ./ Second distillation - bonne chauffe - cognac or brandy production - running time: around 14 hours.

First Distillation

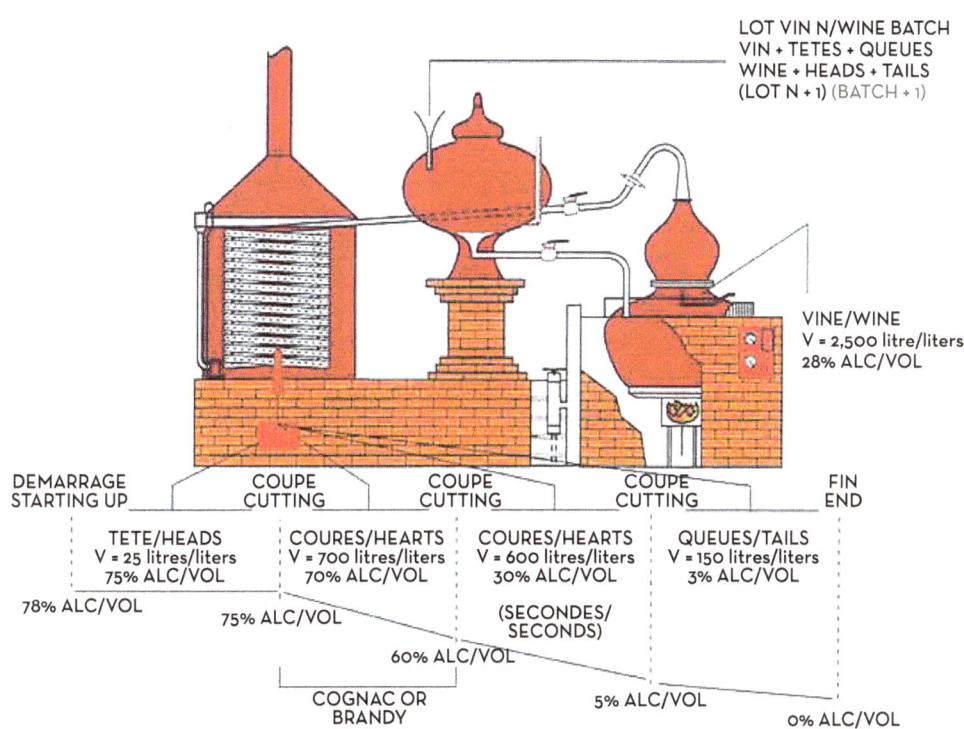

Fig 10b: Seonde distillation - bonne chauffe - production de cognac ou de brandy - temps de fonctionnement 14 heures environ./ Second distillation - bonne chauffe - cognac or brandy production - running time: around 14 hours.

Second Distillation

[27]

Distillation

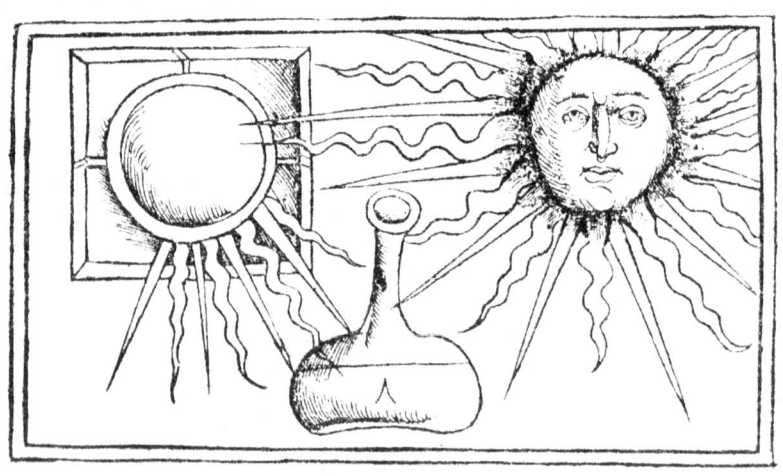

Generalities Of Distillation

The traditional and ancestral double distillation method allowed the distiller to really craft his or her art. By conducting slow distillations with gentle boiling, you obtain the best conditions for rectification. Clean cuts and precise selections of the different components will result in more finesse and complexity.

Distilling continuously for a longer period (a week or more) gives you a better opportunity to make adjustments in the settings of your runs. Because of its simplicity, the alambic pot still needs more attention and is more delicate to operate than a continuous still.

The alambic charentais, usually associated with Cognac, has the ability to produce a good many distillates, such as grapes, apples, pears and other fruit, grains, whiskeys, rums, gins, vodka, etc. With the addition of the fruit basket inside, a mixer in the pot, or a coil inside for steam, you can distill liquids that contain more solids.

First Distillation

When you begin the first distillation using cold wine, it will take more or less an hour and a half from the start to the boiling point, depending on the alambic's size.

Day Run

The day run for the first distillation should have the wine already in the pre-heater. The wine in pre-heater should not be too cold, and the pot should have some head space. If the distiller comes in to the distillery early enough in the morning, he can open the three-way valve right away to warm up the wine.

The wine should not have lees for the day run, since it is shorter than the night run. The day run will run approximately eight to nine hours. Also, because it is shorter, the wine will produce a lighter, more neutral brouillis.

The temperature of the brouillis needs to be somewhere between 13 and 15 degrees C. It is important that it not be colder or warmer than this. When the steam reaches the lower part of the swan neck, turn down the burner so that it is burning very slow. How much you turn down the burner will depend upon the shape and the size of the still, the hat, the swan neck, and the nature of the wine, as it might be foaming over.

Heads

When the heads first start to come over, take off the first few liters of them until the serpentine coil in the condenser is clean and the distillate has lost the overwhelming character of fatty acid and other volatiles. Note the brouillis will always be slightly cloudy.

Brouillis

Increase the heat from the burner slowly to avoid *poulinage*. This occurs when wine and foam are coming directly through to the porte alcoholmeter. Continue to increase regularly, little by little, every half hour until you reach 40% volume on the alcoholmeter and there is more head-space in the pot. Once you have reached 40% alcohol volume, fill up the pre-heater with the next batch of wine. Because of the possible danger of burning, the wine should have no more than four to five percent of lees. The length of time for pre-heating will depend on the length of the coil inside the pre-heater. You will also want to stir the lees about every one half hour, so that the temperature of the wine is uniform from the top of the pre-heater down to the bottom. Pre-heating should be no more than 120 degrees F.

After you have reached 20 percent alcohol volume and there is more head space in the pot, you can then increase the burner more and more in order to reach 70 to 80 percent of full speed.

Tails

If there are defects in the wine, you should take off some of the tails when you reach about three to four percent at the alcoholmeter. Another reason to take off some tails is because when the wine or cider is low in alcohol, such as around eight to nine percent by volume or lower, the alcohol percentage in the brouillis will be raised to 26 or 28 percent by volume.

On the other hand, if the wine is high in alcohol, you should not take off any tails. In this case tails should be taken off only if there are defects. You can add pure water (rain water is best) to have a brouillis under 30 percent by volume.

Because of the faster daytime distillation, you can expect to have less quantity of brouillis, but a higher degree of alcohol.

Night Run

The night runs will always involve wine, since you do not have to be present to watch over them.

Pre-heat the wine in the pre-heater to 45 degrees C, but no more than 50 degrees C. The pre-heating should not last too long in order to avoid "cooking" the wine. As stated above, the wine should be well mixed and the temperature kept even throughout the pre-heater so that there are not cold lees going into the hot pot still. If the lees are not well mixed, then the result could be a brouillis with a burnt or toasted character.

Once the pre-heating is completed, it will take 45 to 50 minutes to reach the boiling point. This is about half the time it would take with cold wine.

When the steam is just at the base of the swan neck, drop the heat to a slow level so that the vapors take 15 to 20 minutes to reach the alcoholmeter. Again, this amount of time will depend on the size and shape of the still.

Heads

Based on using a 25-hectoliter still, six to seven liters of heads should be taken off in order to lose the very strong, pungent smell. Because of the fatty acid in the lees, blue copper-colored particles will come over with the heads.

Brouillis

Once you have collected the heads, raise the flame progressively. Adjust the burner for the night within the equation between the amount of pure alcohol in the pot still and the desired length of distillation. If it is following a short wine distillation during the day, the run could take more than twelve hours. The result will give you a rich, spicy brouillis with a good structure, and a noticeable, heavy and creamy side. This is especially true if the wine had lees and/or a malolactic fermentation.

Tails

Unless the wine is low in alcohol or has defects, you should not take off any tails. Discard all the lees if the wine is mediocre and increase the proportion of heads you are taking off in both distillations.

Second Distillation: The Bonne Chauffe

Because the brouillis contains a lot of fatty acid (more with the distillation of lees, and even more with malolactic fermentation), it should be very well mixed and agitated with a *rouable* before taking a sample and pumping it. Brouillis is never pre-heated, so as to avoid a loss of alcohol.

If you are going to do a second distillation after the first distillation from the night, you should stop the cold water going in the condenser immediately in order to raise the temperature in it. It should take about one-and-a-half hours to reach a boiling point. When the vapors reach the base of the swan neck (it varies depending on the shape and size of the alambic), immediately turn down the burner to a simmer level in order to have the right speed for the obtention of the heads. This level is to be determined by knowledge and experience of the distiller.

HEADS

The amount of heads you collect should be somewhere between 1.5 to 2 percent volume in the pot. The decision is based on different factors: 1) Quality of the wine and the brouillis; 2) How aromatic the varietal is; and 3) How long you plan to age the EDV.

The speed of *coulage*, or the speed of the obtention, is about one liter per minute for 25 hectoliters. It will be a lot less for a smaller pot. The temperature of the heads should be at least 16 degrees C. If the heads are too cold, you can drain cold water from the base of the condenser until you are at 17 degrees C. Because of the very low setting, the temperature of the heads will take a long time to increase to the right level.

EDV

The heart of the bonne chauffe should come more or less in about 6 hours, depending on the varietal and the quality of the grapes. The obtention of the EDV should between 17 degrees to 19 degrees C. If the obtention if colder, it will make the EDV harder. Above 19 degrees C will increase evaporation at the alcoholmeter.

Your distillation should undergo a curve of slowly rising heat, with a peak at about two-thirds. This will take about four hours. Then, you will come down gradually at the double of the setting of the heads.

Some adjustments have to occur in order to obtain an EDV

that is either more neutral or that has more structure. Those decisions are very important. They will influence and determine the true character of your final blends, and the image of your distillery. A cautious experience, keen observation, accurate notes, and many tastings of samples together with other distillers or experts will clarify your vision of what to achieve.

But always remember, you cannot go back in time after your distillation. Like raising children whose character is established in the first three years of their lives, you will have to raise your EDVs to achieve balance and harmony during the aging process and until they reach maturity.

The Historic Moment Of "Making The Cut"

In the last hour before the "cut," you should gradually lower the temperature of your distillate toward 16 degree C to prepare yourself for the *secondes*, which you gathered between 13 at 15 degrees C. It is easier to do because you are reducing the flame of your burner at that time.

How to determine the time to make your cut can be achieved in different ways:

1. "The Three Pearls"

In ancient times, distillers relied on their visual observation to make the cuts. At the fateful moment, you will notice that if you cover your hand over a glass and agitate the spirit inside, a myriad of bubbles float around the inside of the glass. They disappear rapidly, then less and less. When you repeat the same procedure and you only have two bubbles left together and one on the side, and they remain in the glass for a little longer, you have "The Three Pearls." This is beautiful and fairly accurate for grape distillations.

2. "The Nose" Of Cyrano

This method is the mother of the others. The education and training of your nose should drive you in your decision. A long experience in the distillation of grapes, fruits, grain, and plants will increase your accuracy and confidence. Good training is crucial.

In Cognac, at the Organisation Economique du Cognac (ORECO), they created classes on tasting for new or experienced distillers, covering the defects in EDVs coming from the grapes, the vinification, the distillation, and the identification of the different terroir of the appellations. By reproducing the same methods and criteria of their parents or mentors, certain to do the right thing, the ORECO instructors wanted to teach how to avoid common mistakes. It has been very effective to raise the quality of distillates.

3. "The Dance Of The Alcoholmeter"

This method is also based on observation. Let's say you have determined that your cut should occur at 60% volume at the alcoholmeter. At a little above 60%, you will notice an up and down movement of the alcoholmeter. After the third time the alcoholmeter rises a little more than 59.5%, it is time to cut. At first you will be hesitant, but soon you will recognize the "pas de trois" dance steps.

4. "By The Book"

The most reliable, secure way to make the cut is to keep mixing the EDV you have in the tank. Take samples every few minutes until the percentage of alcohol you have in your tank is between 70 and 71% alcohol by volume, but not below 70%. Otherwise, your EDV will be tainted by the *secondes*.

The Aromas At The Time Of The Cut

The varietals and the vintage will influence the aromas during the distillation process. The aromas one finds at the time of the cut will be bitter, astringent, and sticky on the palate. Aromas of artichokes and endives will increase rapidly. Be aware of the pastry aroma, which can induce you to err because of its charm. At this point, your EDV is ready for another life in a new world with multiple possibilities: the aging in oak barrels.

The Secondes *And Tails*

Now your cut is done and you will have three-and-a-half to four hours of distillation to cross the finish line. You want the temperature of your distillate to stay under 15 degrees C and it is very difficult to achieve it without refrigerated water because you are increasing the heat and at the same time have less and less alcohol to extract.

The heat increase is gradual but regular every half hour until you reach 40% volume at the alcoholmeter. It's faster after that in order to more rapidly collect the rest of the alcohol. This is a time when you are burning a lot of calories to reach each 1% of volume. After that, it is not worth the expense and the time.

When you have reached 40% volume with the *secondes*, it

is also the time to fill up the pre-heater with the stirred wine with the lees for the night and start pre-heating it. That will help you to cool down the distillate. It is important to remember to mix the wine in the pre-heater regularly and gently in order to have homogeneity in temperature and keep the lees in suspension.

Your *secondes* can be redistilled with the wine, meaning more rectification, or mixed with the brouillis. In the case of mixing the *secondes* with the brouillis, it is undesirable for quality purposes to have more than a third of *secondes* with the brouillis in the pot still. Management is very important for consistency. These days, there is no cut between the *secondes* and the tails, unless there are olfactory problems or there is a need to keep the percentage of alcohol higher in the brouillis mix.

[An Important Rule] Heads and tails from the first or second distillations must be recycled with the wine, preferably during the night distillation because it is slower. Make sure to reserve some room and add them just before charging the pot to avoid evaporation during the pre-heating.

"Art is wine and experience is the brandy we distill from it"
—Robertson Davies

Defects & Their Origins

Defects From The Grapes & Wine

All of these defects are the results of contaminated ingredients or fermentation problems.

- Acidity: surplus of acetic acids
- Sour: surplus of ethyl acetate
- Sulfur: the smell of rotten eggs comes from a late addition of (and/or too much wettable sulfur on the grapes.
- Acrolein: sharp odor and taste of mustard coming from the attack of the glucerin by bacteria, due to the lack of acidity.

Defects From The Distillation

- Copper/bronze: more obvious after a complete cleaning of the alembic. It disappears after one or two months.
- Esters and Aldehydes: not enough heads have been taken off during the bonne chauffe.
- *Secondes*: the cut at the end of the EDV has been made too late, resulting in a pastry smell, vinosity, asparagus and artichoke odors.
- Cooked: overheated by a concentrated boiling point in the pot.
- Burnt: happens with wine overloaded with lees, combined with too much heat (a smell of burned beans), or from a dirty pot.
- Hard: coming from the obtention of the distillate at a temperature that is too cold, or due to too much rectification.
- Burned fat: due to the lack of refrigeration, or too slow of a distillation, a pot too full, or materials that are not clean.

General Advice

here are a number of general principles that are very important to keep in mind. First, you will want to always keep your samples in the dark and cool place, with detailed information on labels. Also, keep a log book on the samples.

- Take and keep samples of brouillis for tasting.
- Take samples of the heads of the bonne chauffe, always at the same time, like every liter or less, depending on the capacity of your still.
- Take samples during the whole bonne chauffe, but do so before you increase or decrease the fire to avoid disturbance.
- Sample every minute before and after the cut in order to refine your senses in order to make better decisions and to perfect your education.
- Be organized and accurate. In doing so, you will be rewarded by saving time and money.
- Certitudes and over-confidence can induce you into making costly mistakes.
- Remember, with distillation you cannot go back. You will have to live with what you distilled.
- Pay attention to details at all levels, and even if they seem ridiculous. This will improve the quality of your products.
- Vigilance, observation, discipline, common sense, good sense of ethic, open mind, humility, and honesty are your guidelines in the adventure.
- Don't be shy of tasting your products and others with all types of experts, amateurs, professionals, writers, sommeliers, master distillers, master blenders, etc. Men, women, or even your dog (if willing)

are all fair game. Surprisingly they will not agree with each other, but will show you different angles depending on their information, education, the humor of the day, character, and sensibility. That will improve the quality of your distillate, and thus your confidence.

In the past when I did tastings with master blenders of the big houses of Cognac, small distillers, and master tasters from the Organisation Economique du Cognac, I was amazed and surprised by their different perceptions and judgments of the samples I brought from the New World. Perhaps because of the constant (and almost only) reference to their own regional products, their preferences were vastly varied and more in touch with their personal senses rather than their professional ones, although it was very interesting and enlightening.

Cleaning the Still

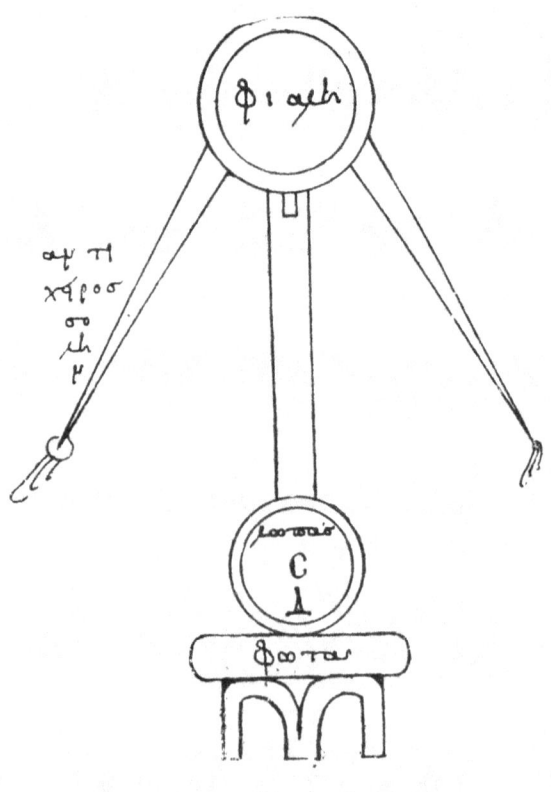

ll the material used for wine, brouillis, heads and tails should always be cleaned properly, immediately after use, and without chemicals to avoid contamination, bad smells of rancid fatty acid and volatile acidity.

Make sure to use different hoses, pumps, and wooden mixing sticks and buckets for the heads, tails, brouillis, and EDV.

You will also need to keep the distillery well ventilated to chase away any foreign odors. The alcohol will absorb them very rapidly.

Don't do any cleaning during the obtention of the EDV, due to the ability of alcohol to absorb odors.

Screen filters of the first distillation should be cleaned with a gentle brush and hot water after each run.

Use thin, unbleached and unscented organic toilet paper on top of your EDV filter.

The pot still and pre-heater should be cleaned after each distillation, especially when distilling on the lees.

Tasting

LA DÉGUSTATION

he evaluation of just-distilled EDV requires many tastings. Many factors can influence your opinion such as the weather, your humor, your perception, mental and/or physical conditions among many other things. So the importance of focusing separately on the different aspects of the distillate (fruit, structure, balance...) will help you to understand and classify the components.

The four senses that are used in tasting are

Sight visual examination of the sample.

Smell evaluation of different odors.

Taste evaluation of different flavors.

Touch feeling, temperature, and aggressiveness of the vapors through the nose and by the mouth-feel of the liquid.

Sight

Sight is the first sense to come into play by noticing the clarity, the viscosity, and the color of the sample. Sometimes it could be misleading for the taster, who could judge the sample severely due to a haze or the color. To avoid any influences in the evaluation of aged spirits, tasters are using colored glasses to mask the color.

Smell & Aroma

Smells and aromas are the most important and crucial sense for evaluation. Smells come through the direct route of the nostrils to reach the olfactory zone in the upper part of the nose. Aroma is the olfactory sensation perceived indirectly by the retro-olfaction when you bring the liquid in contact with the taste receptors on your palate. Then, the heat of your mouth helps to release aromatic vapors to reach the olfactory bulb.

Taste

The tongue can detect four flavors:

Sugar at the tip of the tongue

Acid on both sides of the tongue

Salt in the middle of the tongue.

Bitter detected by the very back of the tongue.

Other sensations are captured and play an important role in tasting: hot, cold, spiciness, etc.

Sensory Abilities And Disabilities Of Individuals

Anosmia The total inability in the perception of odors.

Hyperosmia An abnormal level of olfactory ability, like J.B. Grenouilles in Perfume, by Patrick Suskind.

Heredity This plays an important role, yet is an unquantifiable factor.

Gender The ability to taste is not connected with gender. In fact, the complementariness of the sexes, instead of the opposition, is positive and essential to have complete evaluation of samples. For instance, now days Cognac houses' spirits producers, perfumers, critics, etc, have mixed teams to better understand the tastes of consumers and to generate more creativity and complexity in their line of products.

Age Senses weaken with age. Regular tastings help the taster to keep a high level of efficiency. Long experience compensates for some of the losses in the senses.

When To Taste

The most favorable time of the day is in the morning, from 9 to noon. The senses are well rested and your appetite is growing. You are more alert, sensitive, and have an acute sense of smell.

Culture And Memory

A good memory and past experiences of odors, colors, people, cultures, etc., are constant references for a taster who recollects images, odors and events to identify components. The knowledge of anatomy and descriptive words helps the taster to share his or her comments. It is important to have a good concentration and an open mind when you start a tasting session.

Health And Life

In order to be at his or her optimum sensitivity, the taster should have a healthy life.

- Have regular outdoor activities, such as walking, sports, fishing, etc.

- Have enough rest time, both for your body and mind.
- Eat at regular hours. Food should be balanced, not spicy or too hot. Drinks should not be too strong and imbibed in moderation.
- Do not smoke or eat candy or gum before tastings.
- Do not use perfumes, aftershaves, soaps or toothpastes, etc., prior to tasting. These will interfere with your judgment and the judgment of other people tasting with you.
- Be truthful in your criticism. The first impression is usually the best.
- Try not to take medicines, or at least very little.
- Be curious of other products.
- Taste wines and spirits daily for many years.

Lab Tasting

The room used for tasting should be clear, clean, quiet, and warm, with natural light and no odors. It should also be practical for the taster to take notes during his or her examinations to avoid any distractions.

Make sure to always pour the same quantity of liquid in each glass for comparative tastings.

Glassware

Two types of glasses are recommended. First, there is the tulip shaped glass. This one has more finesse, delicateness and nuance. The tulip glass is also the one that is most favored by experts.

The Liar   The Cellar Master   The Tulip

The cellar master's glass has straight sides and allows aroma to rise more directly to the nose, but it still has a lot of finesse and subtlety.

The sniffer or "The Liar": Never use balloon glasses of any size because the shape interferes with the level of aggression in the alcohol by flattering the senses.

Wash glasses with hot water only – absolutely no detergent.

Taking Of Samples

- A log of samples from your cellars should be taken once a year. Due to the aging process, it is recommended to make sure that your samples are always taken at the same time of year.
- The sample bottles should be clean and rinsed with the samples taken.
- Dark bottles are better.
- Labels should have precise information, such as volume of alcohol percentage, type of fruit, year, origin, yeast, oak, toastage, etc.
- Samples should be kept in dark and cool place.

The Tasting Process

What is a tasting of a spirit? It is an olfactory examination of a product and the sensations (odors) resulting from it. Consider it to be an exploration of the coordination of the product. Classification of odors and perfumes are quite subjective and provisional.

General Characteristics To Note

Appearance

Volatility

Intensity

Depth

Length – in relation to the volatility, but not solely.

Particularities

Aromatics

Flavors

Complexity

Structure

Finish, Also Known As "The Peacock Tail"
    Harmony

    Balance

    Elegance

    Finesse

    Delicateness

Nose

STEP 1: Smell the liquid resting in the glass at different distances, but not too close or too briskly. This will show you the intensity of the sample.

STEP 2: Agitate the glass gently in a circle to increase the surface area of the liquid in order to release more odors.

[Note] to avoid the saturation of your senses, it is recommended to analyze the odors in several passes.

Also, you can cut the sample to 40% by volume with pure water to tame the aggression of the alcohol.

To obtain more information on the less volatile components, you empty the glass, cover it with a glass lid and come back later (from a few hours to several days) to evaluate the residual nose.

Palate: Evaluation Of Taste And Aroma

Absorb a very small quantity of liquid in your mouth, and gently bubble a little bit of air to reach the olfactory zones up in your nose, then spit out the liquid. This operation will help you to evaluate the persistence of the aromatics, and EDV of quality should last at least 30 seconds.

The Origins Of Aromas Of EDV

Primary Aromas The skin and the pulp of the grapes are where the aromatic substances of fruit and flowers reside. They are influenced by the varietal, the nature of the soil, and the microclimate. Due to the fragility of the components, it is important to avoid oxidation of the must and have a clean fermentation.

Secondary Aromas During the alcoholic fermentation of the sugar and also the malolactic fermentation, alcohol, aldehydes, volatile acids, esters, and acetates come in play and are adding to the complexity of the liquid.

Tertiary Aromas With the extraction of components from the oak barrel, the organoleptic characteristics of the EDV go through a transformation. During aging, you notice a slow diminution of the primary elements, and an important modification of the secondary elements. With time and oxidation, the bouquet gains in subtlety and complexity.

Conclusion

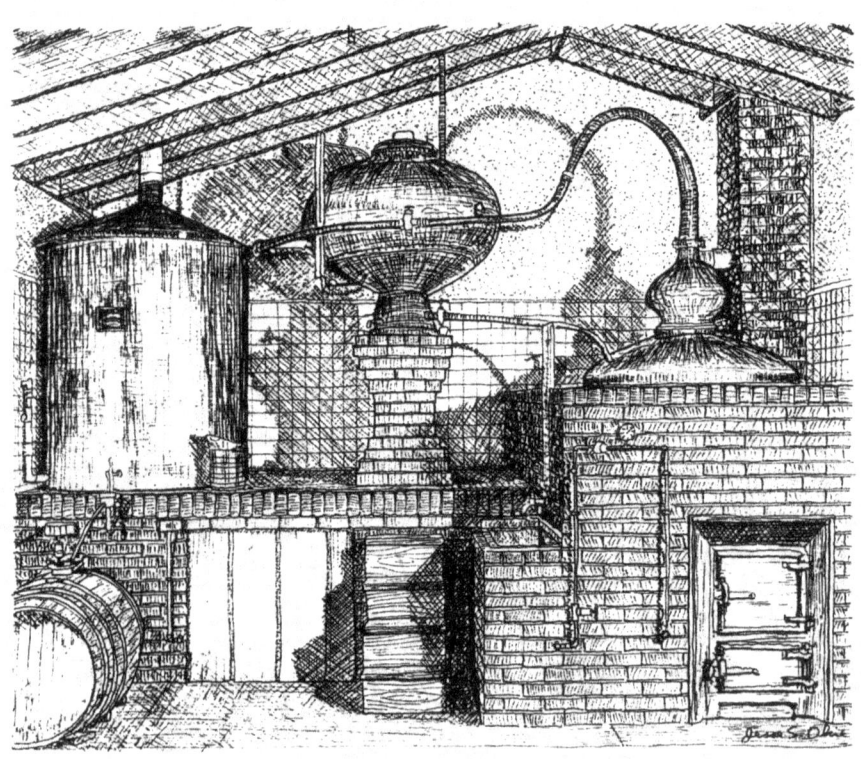

People forgot what emotions were supposed to be.
— Andy Warhol

Distillation is inspiration and creativity; distillation is infinite.
Fall beneath the spell of the ethereal grain of a pear,
Weep tears of joy for a succulent eau de vie of apricot,
Be enthralled by the penetrating acidity of a cranberry liquor,
Be impressed by the deep complexity of a spirit of a venerable age.
— Hubert Germain-Robin

After distillation is complete, the pure *eau de vie* will be either reduced and enjoyed for its freshness and fragrance, or patiently aged in oak barrels for a new life that will be determined by the desire and experience of the Cellar Master.

Aging and blending bring new challenges. They are ancient arts with endless possibilities, a constant research of balance, elegance and complexity.

Alcohol is maybe a double insurance which titillates the genius or consoles to have lost it.
— Hubert Monteilhet, La Part des Anges

Finally, to really appreciate the kindness of alcohol, it should be consumed with moderation and shared with the angels.

Appendices

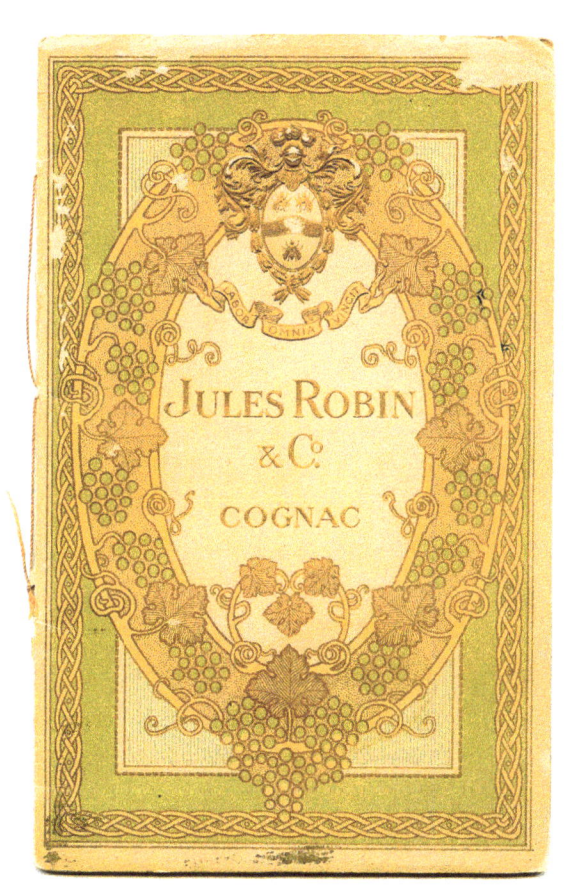

Glossary

WINE

Wine *vin*

Lees, sediments *lies*

Fermentation *fermentation*

Malo-lactic fermentation or ML *malo-lactique fermentation*

Yeast *levure*

Wild yeast (native on the crops) *levure sauvage*

Punch down tool or lees' stirring tool *rouable*

DISTILLATION

Heads (1st part of the distillation) *tetes*

Tails (last part of the distillation) *queues*

Low wine (heart of the first distillation) *brouillis*

Second distillation *bonne chauffe*

Heart of the second distillation *coeur de bonne chauffe*

Water of life *eau-de-vie or EDV*

Seconds (part coming between the heart and the tails during the second distillation) *seconds*

Overflowing (when the wine comes directly to the alcoholmeter holder *poulinage*

ALAMBIC

Alembic *alambic*

Potstill *chaudiere or cucurbit*

Hat *chapiteau or chapeau*

Swanneck *col de cygne*

Condenser, cooler *condenseur, pipe de refroidissement*

Coil *serpentin*

Gas burner *bruleur*

Metric Conversions

LENGTH
1 centimeter = 10 millimeters (mm)
1 inch = 2.54 centimeters (cm)
1 foot = 0.3048 meters (m)
1 yard = 3 feet
1 meter (m) = 100 centimeters (cm)
1 meter (m) = 3.280839895 feet
1 furlong = 660 feet
1 kilometer (km) = 1000 meters (m)
1 kilometer (km) = 0.62137119 miles
1 mile = 5280 feet
1 mile = 1.609344 kilometers (km)
1 nautical mile = 1.852 kilometers (km)

AREA
1 square foot = 144 square inches
1 square foot = 929.0304 square centimeters
1 square yard = 9 square feet
1 square meter = 10.7639104 square feet
1 acre = 43,560 square feet
1 hectare = 2.4710538 acres
1 square kilometer = 100 hectares
1 square mile = 2.58998811 square kilometers
1 square mile = 640 acres

VOLUME
1 US tablespoon = 3 US teaspoons
1 US fluid ounce = 29.57353 milliliters (ml)
1 US cup = 16 US tablespoons
1 US cup = 8 US fluid ounces
1 US pint = 2 US cups
1 US pint = 16 US fluid ounces
1 liter (l) = 33.8140227 US fluid ounces
1 liter (l) = 1000 milliliters (ml)
1 US quart = 2 US pints
1 US gallon = 4 US quarts
1 US gallon = 3.78541178 liters

WEIGHT
1 milligram (mg) = 0.001 grams (g)
1 gram (g) = 0.001 kilograms (kg)
1 gram (g) = 0.035273962 ounces
1 ounce = 28.34952312 grams (g)
1 ounce = 0.0625 pounds
1 pound (lb) = 16 ounces
1 pound (lb) = 0.45359237 kilograms (kg)
1 kilogram (kg) = 35.273962 ounces
1 kilogram (kg) = 2.20462262 pounds (lb)
1 stone = 14 pounds
1 short ton = 2000 pounds
1 metric ton = 1000 kilograms (kg)

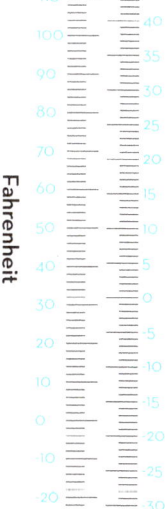

Acknowledgements

To my wife Carole and my sons Alex and Raphael who shared the California adventure with me, and much more.

To my parents Henri and Yolande Germain-Robin, my sisters Christine, Sylvie, Florence and my brothers Jack and Alain who encouraged me in every step of my journey.

To Master Distiller, Yvan Courlit who "sparked in me the passion," for distillation during the fascinating and intense training at the Foundation Fougerat of the Bureau National du Cognac.

To Master Taster Pierre-Alain Gardrat who educated my palate with patience and subtlety in weekly seminars a the Organisaton Economique du Cognac.

To Mr. Lambert, Lucien and Maurice Cabane, Paul Giraud who gave me the confidence and latitude to express myself in the respective distilleries.

To Mr. Renè Firino-Martell (President) and Pierre Frugier, Master Blender and their team who let me explore all the facets of the aging process at the House of Martell Cognac.

To Mr. Robert Prulho for his guidance and his expert advise in my quest of an old alambic pot still.

To Mr. Jean Vicard and his sons Jean-Charles and Jean-Louis for their precious assistance in providing me the old and new quality barrels of any sizes and origins to fulfill my research.

To Dennis Patton of Hidden Cellars who made my first wines in California. I am grateful for his patience and tolerance with my poor English and my constant demands to make wines with unusual specifications.

To Skip Bailey Lovin for his kindness and giving me the opportunity to buy many different kinds of grapes and believing in me.

To the many winemakers and wineries for their continual support: Georges Phelan at Dunnewood Winery, John Parducci, Bobby, Jimmy, John Fetzer and Denis Martin at Fetzer Winery, Bill Crawford at McDowell Vineyards, Michel Salgues and Arnaud Weyrich at Roederer Estates and many others.

To all the growers for their trust and their friendship when a handshake still had the value of a contract.

To all my friends in France and the USA for their precious

support in my never ending quest.

To Nancy Fraley for her wise advice and enthusiasm in putting things together. Without her experience this book would have been impossible.

To Daniel Farber, a fellow distiller who has shared my passion and commitment for the last 25 years.

To Bill Owens, for his knowledge of artisan distillation and his constant research in pursuit of quality, for the enjoyment of consumers.

To Gail Sands, graphic designer, who helped in the creation of making this book a reality.